Rev. Demetrius
Augustin Gallitzin
and the
Catholic Settlements
in Pennsylvania
by
Revue Générale
1865

St Athanasius Press

ISBN-13: 978-1542482585

ISBN-10: 1542482585

St Athanasius Press
melwaller@gmail.com

(email is the best way to reach us)

Rev. Demetrius
Augustin Gallitzin
and the
Catholic Settlements
in Pennsylvania

The events of which the United States
have, during late years, been the theatre
of action, have revived in the recollec-
tion of the editors of the Historisch-poli-
tische Blätter of Munich the name of Loretto, a small and unpretending town of
Pennsylvania, the founder of which was
Prince Demetrius Angustin Gallitzin, the
son of the remarkable woman of whom
Germany has a right to be proud. The
occasion has suggested to them a bio-
graphical sketch, which, full of interest
and appositeness, will unquestionably
be read in Belgium and France with as
much avidity as in Germany.

Twenty years have elapsed since Prince

Gallitzin, who had exchanged the luxuries of princely courts for the poverty of those who herald the glad tidings, slept in the Lord, after forty years of apostleship in the wild regions of the Alleghany mountains. The work set up by the pious missionary yet remains, marked by all the elements of thrifty life, and the little oasis will long continue to be what it was at its origin—the cradle of a Christian civilization, which will go on spreading its blessings to the remotest boundaries, still retaining the unobtrusive modesty which moved its founder's thought. Indeed, had the matter rested with Gallitzin's own wishes, his very name would have passed into vague tradition in those extended regions. It might even have slept in oblivion; for the prince, so careful was he to avoid anything that could attract the attentions of the world, lived and exercised his holy ministry for many years under the borrowed name of Schmidt.

In Father Lemcke, however, and fortunately too, a canon of the abbey of the Benedictines of St. Vincent in Pennsylvania, was found a man who, better than any other, had it in his power to preserve the reminiscences of the noble missionary, and accurately to depict for us the traits of his manly character. Not only did the biographer of the prince know him personally, but he was also his friend, his confidant, his confessor, and his co-laborer in the missions. After Gallitzin's death, Father Lemcke came into possession of his papers, letters, and memoranda, which supplied him with desirable data on the period of life preceding their ministerial connection. He, and he alone, therefore, was in a condition to write a true biography of the prince, and he deemed it a duty to rescue from oblivion the memory of this distinguished man. In connection with this subject, Father Lemcke indulges in a judicious remark: "The life of Gallitzin," says he, "is so intimately inwoven with the events which occurred during his own times, that it holds out to future generations an interest like to that which is offered to us in the life of a Bonifacius or of an Ansgarius, by reason of the facts which have characterized the epochs in which they lived."

Gallitzin belonged to the phalanx of missionaries who, in the United States, scattered the seeds of spiritual life. When the prince stepped on the soil of that vast territory, there was but one prelate, Rt. Rev. John Carroll of Baltimore, the first bishop of the United States, who, from the circumstances of the Church, had been obliged to seek Europe for his episcopal consecration. [Footnote 23] He had been but two years installed—from

1790—and had but uncertain and broken intercourse with his flock. His surroundings, restricted in numbers, but devoted to the holy cause, were mainly composed of, French priests. In this infant church Gallitzin was the second priest consecrated by the Bishop of Baltimore, and missioned, as a true pioneer of civilization, to carry the cross through the untouched forests of the New World, There is an unvarying likeness in all great undertakings; yet it required but a short time—a relatively short time—considerably to increase the number of those men who had devoted themselves to the task. In contrast with the bishop, who, in the course of five years, could ordain and rely on two priests only to feed the flock of the Lord, "The Catholic Almanac" of the day exhibits to us, for the United States, seven archbishops, thirty-six bishops, and four apostolic vicars, with the ministry of two thousand priests, with the addition of convents of various orders, of seminaries, of colleges, of numberless benevolent institutions, with over 4,000,000 of Catholics living under the protection of the laws, in the practice and enjoyment of their faith.

[Footnote 23: There are new details on this distinguished man in a recently published work: "Die Katholische Kirche in den Vereinigten Staatm von Nord Amerika," etc., etc. Regensburg. 1864.]

The Germans delight in recalling to mind that one of those who helped to lay the foundations of the Church in North America was the offspring of a princely house of the Fatherland. Gallitzin was a German on the maternal side; and the noble parent could well claim both the spiritual and natural motherhood of her son, the latter of which was, perhaps, glory enough. How magnificent a mission was that of Princess Amelia Gallitzin! While gathering around her circle the choice spirits which seemed destined to keep bright the torch of faith in Germany, and its living convictions in the midst of a superficial society without belief and without its guiding lights, the princess was rearing for the New World a son who was about to turn aside from a career which his birth and his wealth justly reserved for him, and take up the arduous and thankless labors of the apostleship. This very son it was who, through the work of faith, was destined to be the founder and civilizer of a now flourishing colony.

Strangely enough, nothing in young Gallitzin gave earnest of such a vocation. His almost feminine nature had marked him for a timid, shrinking child; but what was still worse, and a source of deep anxiety to his mother, to this was added a lack of decision, which seemed so deeply rooted in him that not even the iron will of the princess could, during the course of many years, draw out any perceptible results. We have a letter of the princess of the date of 1790, two years before the departure of Demetrius for America, in which she reiterates on this ground her former complainings, her exhortations, and her admonitions. It is proper, however, to advert that the incipient method of training pursued by the princess herself was not free from defect; for, daring the nonage of her son, she herself wavered and hesitated between various systems of philosophy— a course which necessarily must have drawn her into many an error.

There was, therefore, a defectiveness in the main foundation of the training of young Gallitzin, who was reared in a sort of religious indifferentism. But a complete revulsion took place when, after leaving Münster, the princess was led to rest her convictions, not on this or the other system of philosophy, but on the rock of Christian faith—when, from her relations with such men as Furstenberg and Overberg, she herself had gained a greater degree of firmness and steadfastness. This reacted on the education of the son, in the greater decision and authority exerted by the mother; and it was not without fit intention that Demetrius, in the sacrament of confirmation, received the surname of Angustin.

Born on the 22nd of December, 1770, at the Hague, where his father, a favorite of the Empress Catherine, was accredited as ambassador of Russia, young Gallitzin saw before him the opening of a career bound to lead to the highest dignities of either military or administrative service. Nothing, therefore, was spared in giving him a complete education, according to the requirements of the world. This education, developed and closed under his mother's eyes, must be perfected by travel; but whither to direct it was a question of moment. The aristocratic banks of the Rhine were ravaged by the revolutions and war had converted Europe into a vast battle-field. It opportunely happened, at that time, that a young priest, by the name of Brodius, whom the princess had known through the family of the Droste, and who had been admitted to her circle, was about crossing the Atlantic as a missionary to America. The princess had had occasions to value the rare endowments of this priest, and knew how justly her confidence in him could extend. She therefore proposed to him the companionship of her son in a journey which seemed to her to be the only practicable one warranted by the times. The princess, fortunately, met with no opposition on the part of the prince, her husband. An admirer of Washington, and still more so of the philosophic Jefferson, he readily agreed that his son should devote a couple of years to a visit to the United States, so as to judge for himself of the institutions all that country. He earnestly charged him to be introduced to these two great men; while the princess on her part armed him with a letter of recommendation to the Right Reverend Bishop Carroll.

In August, 1792, when twenty-two years of age, young Gallitzin took ship at Rotterdam on his way to America. No one could, certainly, have then stirred him with the idea that the land of America was marked out as a theatre for the evolutions of his existence. Was there a presentiment in that parting hour which, he could not know, was to mark an eternal farewell? Was it a last return of the original indecision of character which made him linger at the roadstead to which his mother had accompanied him? No one can now tell; but what we can say is that when, on the crests of the foaming billows, he caught sight of the yawl which was to carry him on board, his heart failed him, and he turned back to retrace his steps. Then did his mother turn back to him and, with a look of disappointment, "Dimitri," said she, "I blush for thee"—and, grasping his arm, she urged him on to the boat. In a moment, and how no one could tell, the young prince was engulfed in the waves. As quick as thought the practised hands of the sailors fished him up from the waters, and wafted him to the vessel that was to bear him away. Such was his farewell to Europe; but this sea baptism had regenerated him into a new man, as, at a later period, he told the story to his biographer.

On the whole, a noted change had taken place in young Gallitzin. In him every weakness and every irresolution had disappeared, and made room for a firmness, a determination, and an inflexibility which, to his family, became a source of greatest astonishment. Two months had hardly passed by in the intimacies of life with the Bishop of Baltimore, when he already felt, within himself, what soon became a clearly defined resolve. With the close of the year 1792 he wrote to Münster that he had devoted himself, body and soul, to the service of God and to the salvation of souls in America. He wrote that this resolution had been determined by the urgent call for laborers in the vineyard of the Lord; for in the country in which he was then sojourning, his priests had to travel over a hundred and fifty miles of territory, and more, to bring to the faithful the word and the means of salvation.

These were the first news of him received in Münster, and they were disseminated with the rapidity of lightning. From all sides sprang up objections, doubts, and remonstrances against the scheme of the young prince and the boldness of his undertaking. His mother, however, who had at first been alarmed and steeped in agony at the idea of such a vocation, soon reasserted her unerring judgment, and looked into the matter with her wonted greatness of soul. From the moment that, from letters of distinguished persons, and especially from those of the Bishop of Baltimore, as well as from those of her son, she became satisfied that his was a real and substantial calling, she felt perfectly secure, and all human considerations vanished from her sight. She therefore wrote to Dimitri that if, after having tried himself, he was sure that he had really obeyed his vocation, she willingly accepted the reproaches and troubles which could not fail to shower upon him; and that, for herself, she could not desire a consummation dearer to her heart—a greater reward— than to see the child of her affections a minister at the altar of God. And, indeed, not light was the burden of reproaches and afflictions which she had to bear for the love of that son—especially on the part of her husband, it was anything but light. Her letters to Overberg more than amply inform us on that subject Gallitzin, however, seemed to have left his European friends to the indulgence of their astonishment. Heedless of his former social relations, in firmness and resoluteness he trod the path which he had marked for himself, and prosecuted his theological studies with such fervency that his superiors, in view of his failing health, deemed it their duty to interpose. After two years of study, however, he became a sub-deacon, and, on the sixteenth of March, 1795, he was ordained to the priesthood.

There was no lack of labor, however, in the vineyard of the Lord, and the young Levite, the second one who came out of the first Catholic seminary in North America, was immediately put to work. At Port Tobacco, on the Potomac, Gallitzin entered his apostolical career. His fervor, no doubt, carried him too far into those proverbially malarial regions; for, stricken down by a spell of fever, he was ordered by his bishop to return to Baltimore, where Gallitzin was subsequently directed to ascend the pulpit and preach to the German population which had settled that portion of the state of Maryland.

The democratic spirit of American manners, which, with its innumerable abuses, had permeated even religions existence itself, was diametrically opposed to the just conceptions of the priesthood and of the organization of the Church which Gallitzin had formed in his mind. For the primitive morals of which he was then in quest he turned to the unsettled portions of Pennsylvania. "I went there," he tells us at a later period, "to avoid the trustees and all the irregularities which they beget. For success, I had no other warrant than the building of something new, that could escape the routine of inveterate custom. Had I settled where the hand had already been put to the plough, my work would have been endangered, for it had been soon assailed by the spirit of Protestantism."

In the apostolic trips which frequently took him into the then far West, on the table lands of the Alleghany range, near Huntington, where the waters of the Ohio fork away from those of the

Susquehanna, Gallitzin had alighted on a settlement made up of a few Catholic families. In the midst of this Catholic nucleus he resolved to establish a permanent colony, which he destined in his mind as the centre of his missions. Several poor Maryland families, whose affections he had won, resolved to follow him; and, with the consent of his bishop, he took up his line of march with them in the summer of 1799, and travelled from Maryland with his face turned to the ranges of the Alleghany mountains. And a rough and trying journey it was;—hewing their way through primitive forests, burdened at the same time with all their worldly goods. So soon as the small caravan had reached its new home, Gallitzin took possession of this, as it were, conquered land; and, without loss of time, all the settlers addressed themselves to the work before them, and worked so zealously that, before the end of the year, they had already erected a church. The following is Father Lemcke's account of the humble origin of this establishment:

"Out of the clearings of these untrodden forests rose up two buildings, constructed out of the trunks of roughly hewn trees; of these, one was intended for a church—the other, a presbytery for their pastor. On Christmas eve of the year 1799, there was not a winking eye in the little colony. And well there might not be! The new church, decked with pine and laurel and ivy leaves, and blazing with such lights as the scant means of the faithful could afford, was awaiting its consecration to the worship of God! There Gallitzin offered up the first mass, to the great edification of his flock, that, although made up of Catholics, had never witnessed such a solemnity, and to the great astonishment of a few Indians, who, wrapped up in the pursuit of the chase, had never, in their life, dreamed of such a pageantry. Thus it was that, on a spot in which, scarcely a year previous, silence had reigned over vast solitudes, a prince, thenceforward cut off from every other country, had opened a new one to pilgrims from all nations, and that, from the wastes, which echoed no sounds but the howlings of the wild beast, welled up the divine song which spoke: 'Glory to God in the highest, and peace, on earth, to men of good will!'"

The cost of this spiritual and material colonization was at first individually borne by Gallitzin. Captain McGuire, an Irishman, one of the early settlers of the country, had acquired 400 acres of land, which he intended for the Church. These he conveyed to Gallitzin, who divided into small tracts the lands, which he had purchased with his own means, and distributed them among the poorer members of his colony, on condition of reimbursement, by installments, at long periods—a condition, however, which, in a majority of cases, never was complied with.

The wilderness soon put on a new aspect. The settlers followed the impulses of the indefatigable missionary, who kept steadfastly in view the improvement of his work. His first care was to set up a grist-mill; then arose numerous out-buildings; additional lands were purchased, and in a short time the colony was notably enlarged.

In carrying out his work, Gallitzin received material assistance from Europe. In its origin, sums of money were regularly remitted to him by his mother; for he kept up a correspondence, which his devotion to her made dear to his heart

In these relations his father took little, if any, interest, as the determination of his son—his only son—had proved to him a source of bitter disappointment. Still he anxiously desired to see him return to Europe. So engrossed, however, was the young missionary by his work, that such a trip seemed next to an impossibility. Several years had thus glided by, when the idea of visiting Europe earnestly engaged his mind.

In the month of June, 1803, he wrote to his mother, in apology for a long silence; telling her that he is seriously contemplating seeing her once more, but that he is trammelled in his desire by the want of a priest to take his place;—indeed, that his work has so grown under his hands, that he doubts whether he will ever again be privileged to clasp his mother in his arms. "I may not think of it," he adds; "my heart is fraught with affection for you, and it seems to me that I should absolutely see you once more, so as to borrow courage to follow the path which is marked out for me in this perverse world." The letters from Overberg are witnesses of the tears shed by the mother, so anxious again to look upon her son, as well as of the unmurmuring mournfulness of her resignation.

The announcement of his father's death again brought up the subject of his visit to Europe. Indeed, his presence was required in the settlement of his inheritance; but now, as before, the joy of once more treading his native soil, and the happiness of embracing his mother, had to yield to what he considered his duty to his infant colony. The just and plausible reasons which he alleges to his mother for his course, allow us at the same time fairly to appreciate the extent of his work, and the hopes built upon its success. Hence he suggests the consideration due to those families that his advice had influenced, for the greater honor of religion, to follow him in the wilderness;—the money obligations, contracted with various friends, who had trusted him with large sums to speed the development of his scheme, and whose confidence, therefore, might be seriously wronged by his departure;—the interests of so many others, who had committed all their worldly hopes into his hands and whom his absence might leave an easy prey to heartless speculators;—and, finally, the pending questions, started by the scheme of erecting into a county the territory to which the lands of the colony belonged. All these motives, to which others were added, were sufficiently weighty to press on the conscience of Demetrius the duty Of remaining at his post. This final resolution his mother learned with the firmness of Christian

heroism. She wrote to the prince: "What-
ever sorrow may have panged my moth-
erly heart at the idea of renouncing a
hope that a while seemed within reach, I
owe it to truth to tell thee that thy letter
has afforded me the greatest consolation
that I can look for upon earth." It is a
touching picture to behold, in the sequel,
this zealous mother continuing her interest in the mission founded by the prince,
and providing for its success in keeping
with the inspirations of her heart. Thus
it was that, through the channel of the
Bishop of Baltimore, she transmitted to
her son a bill of exchange for a considerable amount, a box of books—a treasure
in those days—rosaries for the settlers,
linen for himself and friends, garments,
and even baby-clothes, for the poorer
members of the settlement, sacerdotal
vestments, embroidered by the princess
herself, by her daughter, and by Count-
ess de Stolberg, and, lastly, a magnificent

present, which the missionary during his life valued beyond all price, and with which, in accordance with his wishes, he was laid to slumber in the tomb.

In the meantime Gallitzin's colony, settled in the midst of those wild wastes, had expanded and become a town, to which he gave the name of Loretto, the beginning of which are thus described by our missionary's successor: "The colony was composed of individuals who generally purchased considerable tracts, varying from one to four hundred acres in extent, which they cleared and converted to cultivation. In proportion as the population increased, they gradually emerged from the savagery of the earlier periods, and soon experienced the wants of a growing civilization. The indication of those wants suggested to Gallitzin's mind the necessity of converting the humble settlement into a town. Mechanics, of every useful trade, rapidly gathered around the nucleus—blacksmiths, millers, carpenters, shoemakers, with even storekeepers, and Loretto soon assumed the position which its founder had designed.

"Here, then, stands the town; but, with its new dignity, came a host of vexations. It marked for Gallitzin a period of struggle against every imaginable difficulty, which brought his firmness to the sorest trials, and which indeed might have jeoparded the very existence of his work. In fact, the means of reducing, under the control of a single hand, the heterogeneous components of such a colony was no easy problem to be solved. Gallitzin efforts to bring it under a normal organization had to meet many an antagonizing element, whilst the peculiar American spirit, which had even then permeated those solitudes, reared up obstacles to his scheme. Gallitzin, however, proved unshakable, and exhibited an unbending energy of character. At one time there was an actual crisis in the prospects of the colony. A member of the community, with a fair allotment of the goods of this world, with the excitable American brain and a marked tendency to speculation, suddenly conceived the idea to set up a competition with the growing colony and to lay the foundations of a rival one in the neighborhood. He went to work accordingly, and, with the assistance of a few Irishmen, actually laid the founda- tions of village, which he named Mun- ster, after one of the provinces of Ireland. This rival of Loretto immediately be- came the headquarters of the propagators of light, in other words, of those who had little relish for the zeal of Gallitzin and the inconvenient discipline of the Church. Satisfied not only with putting the prosperity of Loretto in evident peril, the seceders also assailed the character of Gallitzin, and through these means derived an unexpected help. It happened fitly for their purposes that at the time two German vagabonds—one a priest of most questionable character, and the other a nobleman, whom the crime of forgery had driven from the Old World—presented themselves to Gallitzin, and anything but pleased, no doubt, with the welcome which they received, resolved to swell the party of malcontents. With cunning malice, they soon disseminated reports injurious to their countryman, gave a pretended substance to unfounded suspicions, feeding the animosities of the common herd. The fact, also, of Gallitzin's having assumed a borrowed name was a means of shaking the settlers and sowing distrust in their minds. Things went on from bad to worse, and a catastrophe seemed to be imminent, when came the upshot, so much the more ludicrous because the less expected. The Gordian knot, after the expeditious American fashion, was cut by an Alexander who rejoiced in the name of John Wakeland. He was an Irishman, a giant in stature and strength, famed in the settlement as a wolf and bear killer; and in reality one of the kindest men in the world, and one of the hardest to stir from his natural proprieties. These miserable intrigues and base machinations aroused his indignation, and he immediately came to the conclusion to put an end to them by the interposition of the logic of the strong hand. The agitators had concocted a plan, which was devised to extort from Gallitzin some sort of an assent, and the prince could hardly have escaped their intended violence had he not sought sanctuary in the chapel of Loretto. But the mob had merely adjourned their intended excesses; and they were preparing for extreme means to achieve their ends when John Wakeland, brandishing a sturdy hickory in the midst of the infatuated mob, declared that, he would "settle," on the spot, any one who durst threaten the good priest. There was a magical spell in the hickory. The timidly good men, who there, as everywhere else, had shrunk into a circle of impassive inaction, feeling the influence of a sturdy support, borrowed courage from the hour; and had it not been for the interference of Gallitzin, his detractors, to use an American phrase, would have had 'a rough time of it' From that moment, a complete revulsion of feeling took place in behalf of the missionary; while the bishop succeeded in ultimately restoring order and peace in the little parish. He carefully inquired into all the facts, and then addressed to the parishioners a letter which was posted at the church door, and recalled the faithful to the regular order of things.

"Difficulties, however, of another kind, and of a more serious import, waited on Gallitzin. From the death of his father, he had been suddenly cut off from the pecuniary assistance which he had periodically received from Europe. He himself, as a Catholic priest, had been, by the laws of Russia, excluded from his paternal heritage; while his mother, who had exhausted her means in litigations, was compelled to forego the assistance which, from time to time, she had extended to her son. In satisfying his boundless charities, and in the achievements of his plans, the founder of Loretto had somewhat relied on this inheritance, which thus passed away from his hands. This disappointment, therefore, brought upon him a new burden of anxiety and cares. Destitution and poverty might have been easily borne by him; but he could not make up his mind to give up the idea of founding an imposing Catholic colony—to abandon the undertaking which he had initiated—to be compelled to relinquish lands which had been reclaimed by so much toil and so much care—and, especially, to face impatient creditors, who might accuse him of thoughtlessly going into debt, and from such an accusation justify their expression of contempt."

As a crowning development to all of these tribulations, the European mail brought to Gallitzin the news of his beloved mother's death. On the 17th of April, 1806, in the city of Münster, the excellent princess had closed her eyes for ever, comforting her disappointment that she had not been permitted to see her son on earth by the hope that she would surely meet him in heaven. The narrative of the last moments of the Princess Gallitzin, received, by the stout-hearted missionary, through the letters of his sister, of Overberg, and of Count de Stolberg, supplied a fund of inexpressible comfort; but from that hour the temporal claims and requirements of his position bore terribly on his endurance. It required unheard-of efforts to save his undertaking from the burden of indebtedness, and if, at the hour of his death, he quit-claimed the property of the Church and left it free from all and every charge, the blessed consummation came with the sunset of life only, and that, too, after miracles of constant energy. And here, especially, looms up the secondary phase of Gallitzin's character, which had not escaped his father's more searching eye. In fact, and in answer to a letter of his wife, in which she bitterly complained of the inertness of their son, then sixteen years of age, he wrote to her that "deep waters run still; that, to his mind, she misconceives the disposition of Demetrius, and that he is ever running against wind and tide." And indeed, to struggle against the torrent of time and of events was the whole work of his life. And against this torrent he heaved up the bulk of his writings that have come down to us. It is easy to conceive that it required no common reason to induce a man of his temper of mind to write. We have the motive of this reason in the fact that a Presbyterian preacher of Huntington had thought fit to assail and calumniate the Catholic Church as an institution dangerous to the country and to its liberties. Gallitzin immediately took up the pen in answer, and the necessities of the controversy turned him into a polemica writer.

There are in America, no less than in other countries, fanatical sectarians who follow their congenial instincts in sounding the alarm-cry whenever the Catholic

Church marks out new limits of lawful conquest. In this instance, the state was declared to be in peril; but Gallitzin lost no time in confounding the slanderers of Catholicity by the publication of his "Defense of Catholic Principles," which appeared in Pittsburgh in the year 1816. This work, written in English—for the author wielded the English with as much facility as he did the German language, his mother tongue—was, on both shores of the ocean, greeted with success. Father Lemcke made a German translation of the "Defense of Catholic Principles," of which two editions were published in Ireland and four in the United States, ranking "in popularity with 'Cobbett's History of the Reformation,' to which it bears a resemblance in putting a probing finger on the plague-spot of Protestantism."

The start being once made, Gallitzin

followed up his first work with other publications of an entirely practical character, directed against certain prevalent moral diseases of the day, which mark an epoch in the monography of American ideas. Gallitzin was perfectly familiar with the mode of treatment of the feverish exuberance of American notions, and he handled them with all the cautious skill of a prudent practitioner. Everything which he published on these matters, both in elucidation of his views and as a muniment against the evils which he denounced, is written in the winning and popular style which was familiar to his pen. Hence his works were crowned with success, even amongst the higher classes of society. "Gallitzin's publications," says his biographer, "exerted an immense influence in the period when he lived, but especially so among the humbler members of the community, for whom they were destined. They were found, and they may still be found, in the form of unpretending pamphlets, in the hotels and steamboats of the West, for he had them printed at his own expense and distributed as the Protestant colporteurs disseminate their Bibles and tracts. The curiosity of the readers enlarged their circulation everywhere; and I myself have found them as perfectly thumbed as any spelling-book in spots where I never dreamed of meeting with them."

In the meantime, Gallitzin, who had hitherto labored under the protecting shadow of his humility, had begun to attract the attention of the American world around him. The manner in which he had marked his entrance in social life—not so much by the power of genius as by that integrity of character which commanded the respect of public opinion—had carried his reputation far beyond the limits of the frontiers, and secured for him an esteem, the proofs of which came back to him in numerous testimonials gathering from all sides. It was at this time that he published various pamphlets signed with his real name: "Demetrius Augustin Gallitzin, Catholic curate of Loretto."

It was natural, when the question of creating a new bishopric came up, that all eyes should turn to such a man as Gallitzin. There was a desire, therefore, more than once expressed to see him called to the episcopal chair; but he persistently repelled the intended dignity, and exerted his every power to counteract the efforts of those who were anxious to have it conferred upon him. He asked for one favor only—that of remaining at Loretto; and, with this view, he consented to accept the functions of vicar-general to the Bishop of Philadelphia, which had been recently raised into a diocese.

Since the earlier period when Gallitzin entered on the discharge of the holy ministry, those regions had witnessed a great development of the Catholic faith. From all sides arose new parishes, while the field of labor went on enlarging under the tireless zeal of our missionary. "It may be safely affirmed," says his biographer, "that during the protracted years through which he administered to the district of country which now constitutes the sees of Pittsburg and Erie, he filled the place and discharged the duties of a bishop." In order to form a correct judgment as to the importance of his labors, we must go back, in imagination, to the exordium of the Catholic Church in those countries, where the pastors were cut off from all sustaining advice—from all diocesan organization—and where elements the most discrepant, and prejudices the most stubborn, were found in daily conflict. How many difficulties,

therefore, to be encountered and over-
come in the discrimination, in certain
cases, between falsehood and truth!
What prudence of action was required!
How many and delicate problems presented to the decisions of a tender conscience! Gallitzin, however, was the man
for the situation. "The writings," says
his friend, "which his charge as vicar-
general had compelled him from time
to time to publish, bear witness not only
to his vigilance and zeal, but also to the
great charity which characterized the
performance of his duties." His was a
peculiar solicitude for the persecuted and
the oppressed, because he knew from
experience how readily, in America,
they may be made the sport of falsehood, of malevolence, and of that thirst
of revenge which exists everywhere.
Hence the not inconsiderable number of
persons, both ecclesiastics and laymen,
who looked up to him for protection,

and who might, but for its interpositions, have been for ever lost. His benevolent bearing won for him the confidence of the other priests who, like himself, had consecrated their lives to the salvation of souls. The pastor who from among them became at a later period the archbishop of Baltimore, having been in 1830 appointed coadjutor and administrator to the diocese of Philadelphia, immediately wrote to Gallitzin—whom he styled the propagandist of the faith—to ask the assistance of his experience and of his prayers, and to advise him that he not only confirmed his existing powers, but that he also authorized him to use, without the necessity of any previous application, those with which, as coadjutor, he was himself invested. These two men were bound till death by the closest ties of friendship.

All of Gallitzin's actions were stamped

with the characteristics of candor and uprightness. Should the honor of the Church, or the dignity of her priesthood, be called into question, he knew no such word as compromise. He shrank from familiarity with that species of half education of which presumption is a leading feature; and ever, and everywhere, stood unshaken in his love and assertion of truth—a persistency which, on more than one occasion, called down upon him the imputation of an aristocratic and domineering spirit. Those, however, who, admitted to the closer intimacies of his life, were best qualified to judge, soon became convinced of the futility of the charge. If there were any note of distinction about him, it was to be traced in the loftiness of his conceptions; for he had long cast off all princely frippery; and the privileged society in which he especially delighted was that of the poor and the lowly, with whom he would kindly converse after possessing himself of their wishes and needs. In the circuit of his missions, it was his pleasure to pass by the dwellings of opulence and seek the hospitalities of the humble cottage. There would the prince sit down to rest, surrounded by joyous children, distributing pictures among them and sharing in their humble fare.

Such was Gallitzin, shepherd of souls, polemic and vicar-general, at Loretto, whence the peaceful work of Christian civilization went on quietly progressing and gradually enlarging the circle of its benefits. Years had thus passed on, and the pioneer could already mark the slanting shadows of declining life, when a young missionary came over from Europe to share in his toils. This was Father Lemcke, a Benedictine, who, after having been his assistant, became his successor. Gallitzin was then sixty-

four years of age. Father Lemcke has
left us a picturesque account of his first
meeting with the venerable missionary. He had set out from Philadelphia,
and after several days of rough traveling
reached Münster, where an Irish family
gave him hospitality. From that village
he procured a guide, and at this point of
his narrative we find him with an Irish
lad piloting him to Loretto. "As we
had gone," says he, "a couple of miles
through the woods, I caught sight of a
sled, drawn by a pair of vigorous horses;
and in the sled a half recumbent trav-
eler, on every lineament of whose face
could be read a character of distinction.
He was outwardly dressed in a sort of
threadbare overcoat; and, on his head, a
peasant's hat, so worn and dilapidated
that no one would have rescued it from
the garbage of the streets. It occurred
to me that some accident had happened
to the old gentleman, and that he was

compelled to resort to this singular mode of conveyance Whilst I was taxing my brains for a satisfactory solution of the problem, Tom, my guide, who was trotting ahead, turned round and, pointing to the old man, said: "Here comes the priest" I immediately coaxed up my nag to the sled. "Are you, really, the pastor of Loretto?" said I. "I am, sir." "Prince Gallitzin?" "At your service, sir," he said with a laugh. "You are probably astonished"—he continued, after I had handed him a letter from the Bishop of Philadelphia—"at the strangeness of my equipage? But there's no help for it. You have no doubt already found out that in these countries you need not dream of a carriage-road. You could not drive ten yards without danger of an overturn. I am prevented, since a fall which I have had, from riding on horseback, and it would be impossible for me now to travel on foot Beside, I carry along everything required for the celebration of holy mass. I am now going to a spot where I have a mission, and where the holy sacrifice has been announced for to-day. Go to Loretto and make yourself at home, until my return to night; unless, indeed, you should prefer to accompany me. You may be interested in the visit."

Father Lemcke accordingly followed Gallitzin, and after a ride of several miles they reached a sort of a hamlet, where there stood a good Pennsylvania farm, in which all the Catholics of the vicarage had gathered as on a festive day. The cabin had been transformed into a chapel, and the good people were there, crowding; some standing, others kneeling under the projecting shed; and others again, in small huts or under the foliage of the grand old trees, were awaiting the appointed hour. All had their prayer-books in their hands. At a

sign from Gallitzin, Father Lemcke pro-
ceeded within to receive the confessions
of the faithful; after which the prince
celebrated mass, preached, and administered the sacrament of baptism. For his
pious and good people it was a very festive day. The dinner which followed, and
in which all shared, was a repast marked
by the cheerfulness and the charity of the
agapae of the primitive Christians.

By nightfall both priests had reached
Loretto. On The Sunday following,
Gallitzin introduced his assistant to his
German parishioners, and then, with a
quizzical smile, invited him, without any
further ceremony, to ascend the pulpit.
Father Lemcke had to undergo the or-
deal, and it proved not to his disfavor.
He had naturally supposed that the same
roof which sheltered Gallitzin would
also protect him. The old priest, however, could not see things in that light;

and a few days after, he took him to Ebensburg, the principal county town, and there installed him as the pastor of the parish.

Each of the two missionaries who had thus halved the goodly work still had a respectable circuit to perform. There were stations fifty and even seventy miles apart, and over this immense extent of territory, which now constitutes the Pittsburg and Erie bishoprics, there were, with them, but three or four priests to attend to the work of the Lord. To Gallitzin was reserved the deep gratification of witnessing the branching off, from Loretto, of various Catholic parishes, which were formed in the very manner in which Loretto had been. Twelve miles north of the primitive colony, up to the head-waters of the Susquehanna, where lay cheap and rich lands, some of the more prosperous members of his parish purchased tracts for themselves and their families, and there laid the grounds of a settlement, to which they gave the name of St. Joseph, borrowed from the invocation of the church which Gallitzin had consecrated on that spot. It is now known on the maps as Carrollton. Among the early settlers and the heads of families were sturdy John Wakeland, whom the reader may not have forgotten, and his six sons, as tall and as stalwart as himself, and all, like him, devoted to the Catholic faith. On the very road to Loretto, and before the death of the prince, sprang up a rural parish under the name of St. Augustin. Another was formed with the appellation of Gallitzin—after the death of the missionary, be it understood; for his humility during his lifetime never could have consented to this endowment.

In 1836, Father Lemcke fixed his residence at St Joseph—urged somewhat to this course by Gallitzin, whose favorite idea had, for some time, been to witness on that spot the rise and growth of another Loretto. The old priest, growing into closer intimacy with the younger missionary, periodically came in his sled to St. Joseph, rejoicing to behold "a second edition of what he himself had created thirty years before." So thoroughly had he become linked to this new friend from far-off Europe, that he never but reluctantly parted from him, and even shed bitter tears on once hearing that the bishop contemplated changing Father Lemcke's residence.

Thus was it given to Gallitzin, in the decline of life, to behold trackless forests converted into fruitful fields. The transient cares and annoyances of life had disappeared, and a numerous Catholic population grew around him in the joys of contented toil. The early settlers who with him had shared the sweat and borne the burden of the day, had long bidden farewell to their humbler log-cabins. Well appointed farms, substantial barns, commodious dwellings, surrounded by beautiful gardens and smiling meadows, wooed the eye as the rewarding product of their privations and their toils.

In 1839 the old missionary's health began to fail. The load of years much less than the thousand hardships inseparably connected with the devotions of apostolic life, weighed heavily on a frame attenuated indeed, but still erect and resisting. Yet the burden went on pressing still—the body gradually bent—the step unsteady—the divine fire which always kindled still animated him; but the voice would refuse the assistance of its sounds, and the close of his sermons turn into a peroration of silent tears a thousand times more eloquent then his spoken words. And yet, with all these warnings, he rejected every suggestion of precaution and care of himself. To this he would answer, in his own energetic language, that "as the days had gone by when, by martyrdom, it was possible for us to testify to God's glory upon earth, it was our duty, like the toil-worn ox, to remain hitched to the plough in the field of the Lord." And the event harmonized with his wish. On Easter Sunday, 1840, Gallitzin, being then seventy years of age, had early in the morning taken his seat in the confessional. After the discharge of its duties, he had braced up the remnants of his strength to ascend the altar for holy sacrifice. He was, however, compelled to forego the sermon of the day to betake himself to his bed, from which he was destined never again to rise. The attentive care of Dr. Rodriguez, his intimate friend, prolonged his existence for a few weeks; but it was soon ascertained that the noble missionary was fast sinking under exhausted energies. With the rapidity of lightning, the sad news was carried abroad. From far and near, old and young gathered around his dwelling, once more to receive the blessing of the man whom they revered. So great was the affluence of the people, that in order to secure a few quiet moments for the glorious veteran of faith, absorbed in the last meditations and prayers of earth, it became necessary to warn away the increasing throng of visitors—and this without his knowledge; for it was his wish to receive every one of them, and to each to speak the last farewell which welled up from his loving heart. Yet some did come for whom no such words passed his lips, which on the contrary moved in utterances of reproof and blame. Among others came in one of the parishioners, to whom the dying pastor had been particularly kind. He, however, had proved ungrateful, and had, indeed, been a cause of much annoyance to the missionary by habits of drunkenness and other excesses of an unregulated life. As he entered the room, the venerable pastor turned to him with a reproachful look and shook his head. This silent sermonizing produced a deeper impression than had any previous admonition of Gallitzin. The self-accusing culprit fell upon his knees, melted to tears, confessed his errors, and promised thenceforward to amend. The evidence of his sincerity is found in the statement of Gallitzin's successor, who informs us that he stoutly held to his promise.

The last scene of this eventful life closed on the sixth of May, when the missionary prince left this world, accompanied by the prayers of his parishioners gathered around him; for every apartment of the house, and every portion of the chapel attached to it, was literally thronged by a wailing, weeping, and praying community. This supreme hour revealed the depth and the sincerity of the love which dwelt in every heart for this man of God. On the day of his burial, whole populations swarmed from every point—from distances ranging fifty and sixty miles—to pay to the good father a last tribute of that affectionate respect which had attended him through life.

The most respectable men of the parish contended for the honor of bearing his body to the cemetery. In the body of the church, it was a perfect contest among the congregation to look for the last time on the feature of him who was thenceforward for ever lost to earth. Those who were lucky enough, through the pressure of the crowd, to reach the coffin, kissed in tearful love the icy hands of the missionary; while the attendants were compelled to resort to force in order to close the coffin for the final rites of the Church.

It were no easy task, without reference to the work of his biographer—an ocular witness of Gallitzin's labors—to convey a just conception of their bearing and extent "When," he says, "we come to consider the theatre on which Gallitzin inaugurated his immense labors in so obscure and modest a manner, we realize the amount of substantial good that can be achieved by an apostolic missionary in America when, like Gallitzin, he conceives the practical sense of things and leads them on to their crowning development with the zeal and perseverance which marked his course. The small county of Cambria, in Pennsylvania, created in 1807, which is indebted to Gallitzin for a majority of its settlers, is everywhere, and with every reason, characterized as the Catholic county. Indeed, when the traveller on business, or the tourist for pleasure, strikes this point from other districts of Pennsylvania more controlled by Protestant influences, it seems to him that he has passed from a comparative desert into a smiling oasis. This may be easily understood. For all their journeyings for whole days, over counties twice and thrice more opulent than this little Catholic county, there is no indication to tell them what religion is there professed. Not till they have pressed the soil of Cambria county do they feel that they are in a truly Christian land, as they catch sight of ten Catholic churches and three monasteries—all of which cropped out of Loretto under Gallitzin's creative and fostering hands."

From all these results we can frame an accurate judgment of the prince's career, which was but one continuous struggle—a glorious struggle, teeming with usefulness. When Gallitzin opened his mission, the vicar of Christ was persecuted and proscribed. A prisoner, torn away from his spiritual family, Pius VI. heard the voices of a philosophic world applauding his abduction, as, ten years later, it applauded the violence inflicted on the person of Pius VII. It was just at that dark period which overshadowed the Holy See that the Church inaugurated her peaceful labors in the United States, and, at the end of ten years, had marked her beneficent influences by a progress so rapid that its result could not escape the eye of even the least observant. While Europe was organizing a settled persecution of the papal power, the Church in America was growing up and expanding in influence. Her very adversaries were compelled to bear even reluctant witness to her triumphs. In one of the meetings of a Bible society some years ago. Lord Barclay exhibited a summary, in which he lamented the spread of Catholicity in a country in which he said that in the year 1790 there was not even a bishop. "Strange," he said, "that while, in Europe, the power of the see of Rome is overthrown, the Pope is a prisoner, and Rome is declared to be the second city of the French empire—strange, I say, that, at this very moment, the power of the Pope should be rooted in America in this still stranger manner." Ay! Strange indeed, my Lord Barclay; but in no way strange for those who know that martyrdom is the life of the Church, and that she woos triumph in persecution. Gallitzin's life is a living, convincing proof of her triumphs and her hopes.